The Child-Owner's Handbook is the definitive Workshop Manual for everyone faced with the problems and costs of running a child. All couples contemplating parenthood, those awaiting delivery of the new baby and the parents with an existing model will find this book an invaluable source of advice and guidance. It provides an easy-to-follow alphabetical list of hints on running and servicing the new arrival, together with detailed definitions (some with the help of diagrams) of all the major technical terms.

The Child-Owner's Handbook

SIMON BRETT

London
UNWIN PAPERBACKS
Boston   Sydney

First published by Unwin Paperbacks 1983
Reprinted 1985
This book is copyright under the Berne Convention. No reproduction without permission. All rights reserved.

UNWIN® PAPERBACKS
40 Museum Street, London WC1A 1LU, UK

Unwin Paperbacks,
Park Lane, Hemel Hempstead, Herts HP2 4TE, UK

George Allen & Unwin Australia Pty Ltd
8 Napier Street, North Sydney, NSW 2060, Australia

© Simon Brett, 1983

British Library Cataloguing in Publication Data

Brett, Simon, 1945–
  The child-owner's handbook
1. Children—Management
I. Title
649'.1   HQ769
ISBN 0-04-827069-5

Set in 11 on 12 point Plantin, by V & M Graphics Ltd, Aylesbury, Bucks and printed in Great Britain by Cox and Wyman Ltd, Reading

CONTENTS

Model Identification	*page*	1
Specifications, Dimensions, Weights and Capacities		3
Wiring Diagram		4
Lubrication Chart		5
Spares and Touring Pack		6
Glossary of Technical Terms (In Alphabetical Order)		9
Appendix I – Naming Your Child		110
Appendix II – At-a-Glance Fault Diagnosis Chart		115

MODEL IDENTIFICATION

The HUMAN CHILD (originally named BABY and subsequently – sometimes – ADULT) has been in production for between 10 and 12 million years, with only minor modifications.

All but the very earliest models (which you are unlikely to encounter outside a museum) usually move on two legs.

There is only a BASIC model available in the range, though the addition of accessories can lead individual owners to claim they have DE LUXE, SUPER, or APPALLING versions.

Outwardly all models can be identified by common distinguishing features (See SPECIFICATIONS), and are available in a full range of colours.

All models have the same fuel-intake, ventilation and exhaust systems. The interior fittings are also very similar.

The only important variation in the BASIC HUMAN CHILD is that between the MALE (MARK I) model and the FEMALE (previously known as the MARK II, but now changed by feminist pressure, to the ANNE I) model. These types can be seen in BABY form in Figs. 1 and 2.

(NB This handbook does not deal with hot rod or customised CHILDREN.)

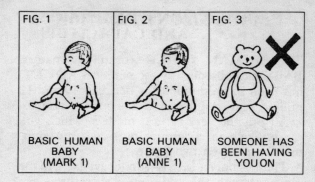

SPECIFICATIONS, DIMENSIONS, WEIGHTS AND CAPACITIES

SPECIFICATIONS

    TORSO   1
    ARMS   2
    LEGS   2
    HEAD   1
       (Incorporating EYES   2
                             NOSE   1
                             MOUTH   1
                             EARS   2)

DIMENSIONS

OVERALL LENGTH }	Huge, bigger than when last seen, according to grandparents.
OVERALL HEIGHT }	
GROUND CLEARANCE	Almost none, especially when ground is muddy.
WEIGHT	Huge, according to grandparents. Not overweight, according to mothers.
CUBIC CAPACITY	Huge (particularly between meals).

WIRING DIAGRAM FOR BASIC HUMAN CHILD
(Types Mark I and Anne I)

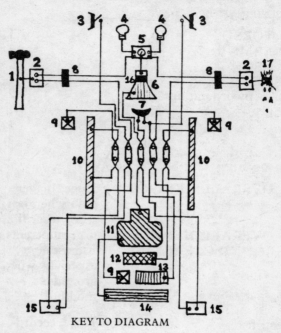

KEY TO DIAGRAM

1. Battery
2. Direction indicator
3. Auditory system (liable to deliberate switch-off, which can lead to blowing of fuse in parent)
4. Warning lights
5. Regulator (rarely used)
6. Hooter
7. Charm circuit
8. Resistance (to having vest put on)
9. Temperature gauge
10. Tickle-sensitive panel
11. Fuel tank
12. Flasher unit
13. Wiper assembly
14. Exhaust system
15. Kick starter
16. Fuel tank level indicator
17. Earth

LUBRICATION CHART
LUBRICATION POINTS AND RECOMMENDED LUBRICANTS

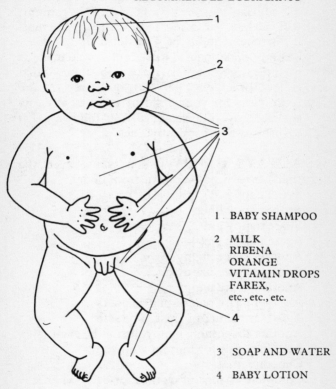

1. BABY SHAMPOO
2. MILK
   RIBENA
   ORANGE
   VITAMIN DROPS
   FAREX,
   etc., etc., etc.
3. SOAP AND WATER
4. BABY LOTION

(NB BABY OIL may also be applied at most of these points, though it is inadvisable to apply it at 2. For advice on frequency of changing a baby's oil, consult an expert.)

SPARES AND TOURING PACK

Before undertaking any journey, however short, it is advisable to check your child and its contents – or the latter are likely to be spilled at the most inconvenient moment. Accidents do happen – indeed *will* happen, and a parent should make all possible preparations to avoid their worst effects. Emergency services, quick repairs and spare parts for your child may not be as easily available as you imagine. The following list covers most basic eventualities.

ALWAYS CARRY (when taking even the smallest baby outside your front door)
Spare nappy
Spare nappy liner
Spare nappy pin
Spare plastic pants
Another spare nappy
Another spare nappy liner
Another spare nappy pin
Another spare pair of plastic pants
A disposable nappy, just to be safe
Another disposable nappy, just to be even safer
Muslin nappy for mopping up vomit
Changing mat
Complete change of clothes for baby when it is spectacularly dirty
Complete change of clothes for self when baby is spectacularly dirty
Polythene bags for debris
Breasts/Bottles (as applicable)

Gripe Water
Cotton Wool
Baby Lotion
Dummy
Rattle
Juice/Baby Food (as applicable)
Spare socks (for baby)
Sterilising tablets
House keys
Pram
Warning triangle (if pram breaks down – compulsory on continent)
Bottle of gin (if parent breaks down – quite likely anywhere)

GLOSSARY OF TECHNICAL TERMS

(In Alphabetical Order)

ADENOIDS – Dot bakes childred tock fuddy.

ADEDOIDS – What children suffering from the above claim to have wrong with them.

ADOLESCENCE – The 'Awkward Stage', the point at which children develop all the characteristics of one's in-laws.

ADVENTURE PLAYGROUNDS – Areas where children feel free to leap around uninhibitedly, bounce on things and knock things over (e.g. Granny's front room, where she keeps the best Wedgewood).

A.I.D. – Artificial insemination by donor.

A.I.H. – Artificial insemination by husband.

A.I.L. – Artificial insemination by lodger. (Well, that's his story, because he swears he wasn't even in the area at the time.)

ALCOHOL AND BREAST-FEEDING – Under no circumstances try to feed breasts alcohol.

ALLERGY – That which distinguishes the spots of a child of middle class parents from those of lower class children.

ALPHABET – It is very important that children should learn their Alphabet as soon as possible, since it is the basis of all reading and writing skills. There are many mnemonic verses designed to help children to master this essential information, but most of them (e.g. 'A was an Archer, who shot at a frog,/B was a Butcher, and had a great dog,/C was a Captain, all covered with lace ...' etc.) bear little relation to contemporary life. To remedy this deficiency, here is a new Alphabet Rhyme, which not only teaches the 26 letters, but also helps to prepare the modern child for the world in which he is growing up:

A was an Accountant, keeping just this side of crime.
B was a Bureaucrat, wasting people's time.
C was a Computer, making pointless calculations.
D was a Doctor (Only Private Consultations).
E was an Economist, floundering in the dark.
F was a Flasher, who paraded in the park.
G had been in Government, but then lost his deposit.
H was a Homosexual, who came out of the closet.
I sold Insurance to all his friends from school.
J was a Jogger, who looked an awful fool.
K was a Kerb-Crawler, making propositions.

L a Local Councillor, with political ambitions.
M was a Minister, ducking issues in debates.
N was a Newsreader, who opened lots of fêtes.
O was an Orthodontist, who could make your teeth all glistening.
P was a Psychoanalyst, with hourly rates for listening.
Q was a well-paid Quango, without a lot to do.
R was made Redundant at the age of forty-two.
S was a Scrounger, who lounged in his pyjamas.
T was a Tax Exile, safe in the Bahamas.
U was Unemployed – just as you'll grow up to be.
V was a Virgin (well, there's a novelty!)
W was a Wrestler, rehearsing every grunt.
X was a Zenophobe, who joined the National Front.
Y was a Yobbo, beating up an O.A.P.
And **Z** a Zymotologist – whatever that may be!

AMNIOTIC FLUID – Literally, the fluid of forgetfulness (cf. Amnesia) – i.e. gin, whisky or anything else that gets the father through pregnancy.

ANAEMIA – One of the less popular Victorian Christian names for little girls.

ANTENATAL CLASSES FOR FATHERS – These evening sessions make the father-to-be *really* aware of what he's done. Large numbers of hugely pregnant wives and sheepish husbands are herded into a room, where they are shown slides of the human reproductive organs to explain why they're at the antenatal class rather than in the pub. Birth is then described to them and various exercises (e.g. giving one's wife Chinese burns to simulate contraction pains) are demonstrated. The climax of the evening is a film of a birth (refused a certificate for general release, but on show at certain cinema clubs catering for special tastes). There is also a question-and-answer session. (If the questions come before the film, there is bound to be a sheepish enquiry from one husband about sexual intercourse during pregnancy; if the questions come after the film, all the husbands suddenly decide they've gone off the whole idea of sex.) Antenatal classes for fathers always finish before the pubs shut, so that the participants can go off and repair their shattered nerve-tissue.

ARTIFICIAL INSEMINATION – All the hard work and none of the fun.

BABY BLUES – Depression following the birth of a boy. (cf. BABY PINKS)

BABY-BOUNCER – A particularly tough toddler who beats up and throws out rowdy elements at children's parties.

BABY BUGGY – Health Visitor's comment (cf. LICE, NITS).

BABYGROS – Of course it does.

BABY-SITTING CIRCLE – A reciprocal arrangement whereby parents seem to spend every night looking after other people's children and then find nobody's free on the one evening *they* want to go out.

BABYTALK – In dealing with this subject, it is important to make the distinction between NATURAL BABYTALK, the language actually used by babies, and UNNATURAL

BABYTALK, the language used by adults when talking to babies. It is significant that babies themselves cannot understand a word of UNNATURAL BABYTALK, but tend to gurgle and smile when addressed in it, because it obviously makes the adults feel better if they do.

Many adults regard a basic grounding in UNNATURAL BABYTALK as essential for all dealings with people under the age of eighteen months, and it is for their benefit that there follows a two-part language course in BASIC UNNATURAL BABYTALK:

LESSON ONE A. *Manner of Speech.*
The important thing to remember is that all UNNATURAL BABYTALK is interrogative. Every sentence is a question, and the fact that none of these questions ever gets answered should not deter the student.

The manner of delivery in UNNATURAL BABYTALK is also important. When speaking the language, the eyes should take on an expression of asinine content, and the lips be firmly puckered. All sounds should be delivered on a note of strangled cooing.

B. *Vocabulary.*
As with most languages, the first priority is to learn the vocabulary, which, in UNNATURAL BABYTALK, is not extensive. For this lesson, students should endeavour to memorise the following columns of basic words. Then they

can move on to sentence structure, a process which is simplified by the layout of the chart. (Any combination of three numbers from 1 to 4 will produce a sentence in UNNATURAL BABYTALK. For example, the sequence 3-2-4 gives the very acceptable enquiry:

IZZENTUMZA UVVI-ICKLE
SAUSAGE-PIE?

Other combinations, of course, produce other sentences.)

LESSON ONE WORD-CHART

1. IZZUMZA	1. BOOFUL	1. BOYDEN?
2. OOZA	2. UVVI-ICKLE	2. GIRLDEN?
3. IZZENTUMZA	3. POOEY	3. BUBBYDEN?
4. WASSAMATTAWIDDA	4. HUNG'Y	4. SAUSAGE-PIE?

LESSON TWO
This follows the pattern of Lesson One, although the vocabulary is now more advanced. Again, memorise the words and use three-number sequences to produce sentences.

LESSON TWO WORD-CHART

1. DUZZUMS-WANTUMS	1. PITTY	1. BOCKLE?
2. WHEREZUMS	2. TEENSIE	2. DINKIE?
3. DIDDUMS-WANTUMS	3. WEENSIE-ICKLE	3. TOOTSIES?
4. WATTA-UVVI	4. TEENSIE-WEENSIE	4. OOJA-WOOJA-WOO

These two lessons cover all one needs to know about UNNATURAL BABYTALK (though students who wish to pursue their studies further are recommended to write to the Open University, who will tell them exactly what to do with themselves).

BABY WALKER – Mr and Mrs Walker's little boy.

BAKED BEANS – See FISH FINGERS.

BEDTIME – There are no fixed rules about the time children should go to bed, but in most families a pattern emerges. The resulting time is usually a compromise between when the children want to go to bed (never) and when their parents want them to go to bed (as soon as they wake up).

BEDTIME STORY – Almost all children like to have bedtime stories read to them. This is an important stimulus to the child's imagination, but can get rather wearing for the parents' patience. There are so many children's books on the market, that it is difficult to know which one to choose. For all parents with this dilemma, here is an all-purpose children's story, which can, with minor variations, be used from the age of eighteen months up to four:

ALL-PURPOSE CHILDREN'S BEDTIME STORY

(Delete where inapplicable)

ONCE UPON A TIME there was a little

{
BOY　　*called*　PETER
GIRL　　　　　　　JANET,
RABBIT　　　　　　WHISKERS,
PONY　　　　　　　PONGO,
SQUIRREL　　　　　NUTTY,
TEDDY BEAR　　　　HUMPHREY,
ELF　　　　　　　　TINKLE,
}

and one day he was walking through the

{
WOODS *and met*　HIS FRIEND JANET.
TOWN　　　　　　HER FRIEND PETER.
HEDGEROWS　　　THE VILLAGE BOBBY.
HIGHWAYS　　　　A GIRAFFE.
LONG GRASS　　　A GIANT.
SLUMS　　　　　　THE VAT INSPECTOR.
}

'Hello,' said the little

{
BOY.　　*'How are you today?'*
GIRL.
RABBIT.
PONY.
SQUIRREL.
TEDDY BEAR.
ELF.
}

'Oh, I'm

{
FINE,'   *replied the other.*
SPLENDID,'
VERY SAD BECAUSE I'VE LOST MY
   MAGIC THIMBLE,'
BORED OUT OF MY SKULL,'
TIRED AND EMOTIONAL,'
PRETTY RANDY,'
}

'In fact, I'm just on my way to see the

{
RABBIT FAMILY.'
WISE OLD WIZARD.'
WISE OLD OWL.'
FAIRY RING.'
TOTAL ECLIPSE OF THE SUN.'
CHELSEA MATCH.'
}

'Oh, can I come with you?' asked the little

{
BOY.   *'I should*
GIRL, etc.
}

love to see

{
HIM.'
THAT.'
THEM.'
}

So together they walked along the

{
ROAD.   *The sun was*
FAIRY PATHWAY.
MAGIC STAIRCASE.
JUVENILE COURT CORRIDOR.
KHYBER PASS.
}

shining and, as they walked, they

> SANG A LITTLE SONG,
> TALKED EXCITEDLY ABOUT THE
>   FAIRY BALL,
> SKIPPED AND JUMPED FOR JOY,
> WHISTLED MERRILY,
> MADE UP RUDE LIMERICKS,

and the time passed very quickly.

When they got where they were going to, the little

> BOY
> GIRL, etc.

said

> 'GOOD GRACIOUS!'
> 'PEPPERED PEANUTS!'
> 'BLESS MY WHISKERS!'
> 'OH, AREN'T I A SILLY-BILLY!'
> 'GAWDSTRUTH!'

because there, sitting on a

> SPLENDID THRONE,
> DONKEY,
> DRAGON-FLY,
> TOADSTOOL,
> BAR STOOL,

was the biggest

- DRAGON
- WIZARD
- FAIRY
- OWL
- CHIMNEY-SWEEP
- DOUBLE-GLAZING SALESMAN

they had ever seen. And, do you

know, in his hand he was holding

- THE MAGIC THIMBLE.
- TWO RAINBOW-COLOURED ICE-CREAMS.
- A SNOW-WHITE DOVE.
- THE MISSING BOTTLE OF FAIRY-DUST.
- THEIR LONG-LOST SISTER.
- A DOUBLE GIN.

'I have been expecting you two,' he said with a

- JOLLY SMILE.
- CHEERY WAVE.
- HAPPY LAUGH.
- DEEP SIGH.
- GLAZED EXPRESSION.

'I thought you'd come back for this.'

And, do you know, he was so kind that, in spite of everything, he gave it back to them before

{
YOU COULD SAY JACK ROBINSON.
YOU COULD BLINK YOUR EYE.
A RABBIT COULD TWITCH A WHISKER.
THE STARS CAME OUT OVER FAIRY-LAND.
THE HIRE-PURCHASE COMPANY REPOSSESSED IT.
FALLING BACKWARDS IN A HEAP ON THE GROUND.
}

So they were reunited and all went off to the

{
FAIRY BALL.
CIRCUS.
FUNFAIR.
LAND OF NOD.
PLACE WHERE ALL GOOD CHILDREN GO.
PUB.
}

And they all lived happily ever after.

ALL-PURPOSE CHILDREN'S BOOK ILLUSTRATION

BED-WETTING – Caused by children in two ways:
   a.   The obvious one (stream of unconsciousness).
   b.   Unexpected bouncing on parents' bed while they're drinking early morning tea (a. is easier to control. Ignore it and it'll go away. Most adolescents come to realise that it doesn't improve their chances of getting members of the opposite sex into bed with them, and give it up. There is no known method of controlling b.)

BIB – A protective garment worn by a child when playing with its food.

BIB-BIB – A protective noise made by a child when playing with its cars.

BIB-BIB-BIB-BIB-BIB-BIB-BIB – a. A protective garment worn by a child with a stammer.
b. The pay-tone of a public telephone.

BINOVULAR TWINS – Non-identical twins, born from two separate eggs. The simplest way of telling binovular twins apart is by looking at them.

BLUE PETER – Usually just a sign of cold weather.

BLUE PETER SYNDROME – A tendency that has been observed in children who watch too many wholesomely instructive children's television programmes. It manifests itself in their language, which becomes irrevocably wholesome and instructive. They speak in patronising voices and begin every sentence, 'What you do is …' (See CRACKERJACK SYNDROME)

BOOKS ON CHILDCARE – There is a considerable industry in the publication of childcare books and few young parents are immune to its influence. The progress of the average childcare library is shown in the diagram opposite.

BOOTEES – These are knitted by Auntees for babees to put on their tootsees and are prettee yuckee.

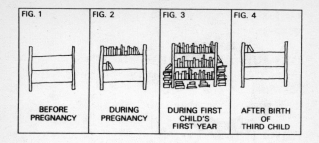

FIG. 1	FIG. 2	FIG. 3	FIG. 4
BEFORE PREGNANCY	DURING PREGNANCY	DURING FIRST CHILD'S FIRST YEAR	AFTER BIRTH OF THIRD CHILD

BOTTOM-SHUFFLING – A form of cheating at cards.

BOWEL MOVEMENT – The bowels tend to move at the same time as the rest of the child; indeed, it is very rare for a child to move and forget its bowels, except in cases of extreme absentmindedness.

BOTTLE – Something greatly appreciated by baby and father.

BREAST – See above.

BREAST PADS – Part of the equipment of women cricketers.

BRAXTON-HICKS CONTRACTIONS – A form of bidding in bridge.

BURPING – An activity passionately encouraged in children until they are weaned, and thereafter equally passionately discouraged.

CAESARIAN SECTION – See LATIN QUARTER.

CAKES – As soon as a child gets to school, if not before, the parent is faced with competition in all matters of juvenile celebration. (See BIRTHDAY PARTIES) Cakes are a part of this; reports from other parties attended make it clear that every other mother in the district is a sculptor of comestibles whose skill exceeds that of Rodin or Henry Moore. ('At Emma's party, her Mummy had made a cake in the shape of a space-rocket/Range Rover/the Galapagos Islands/teddy bear/oil refinery/the Solar System ...' etc.)

NO MOTHER SHOULD GIVE WAY TO THIS PROPAGANDA

Because
a)   Children at parties don't eat birthday cake.

They only like it there so that they can blow out the candles. (All they actually EAT are crisps and sausages.)

b) A failed cake supposed to be in the shape of something will not go unnoticed. ('What is it? What do you mean – a hedgehog? Where are its prickles? Which end's which? That doesn't look like a face to me. Is it meant to be a hedgehog that's been run over? I think it looks more like an oil refinery ...' etc., etc., etc.

c) If you've got to have a cake, it is better to make one that stimulates your child's imagination (*See Diagram*).

Therefore, a really brave mother will dispense with a cake altogether, and just bring in a lump of wood stuck with candles, so that they can be repeatedly blown out. A less brave mother will make one of the following imagination-stimulating cakes:

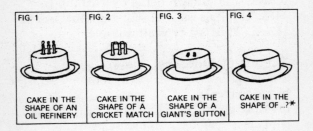

FIG. 1	FIG. 2	FIG. 3	FIG. 4
CAKE IN THE SHAPE OF AN OIL REFINERY	CAKE IN THE SHAPE OF A CRICKET MATCH	CAKE IN THE SHAPE OF A GIANT'S BUTTON	CAKE IN THE SHAPE OF ...?*

*   (A SMALL PRIZE TO BE AWARDED TO THE CHILD WHO COMES UP WITH THE MOST FLATTERING SUGGESTION.)

CAMPING COT – A cot made collapsible for

easy transportation. The average father can assemble one in a mere four hours.

CARDIGAN – Nursing mother's garment, identified by patches of congealed vomit on shoulders.

CARRY-COT – Father of small child going away for weekend.

CASE, FOR HOSPITAL – Since babies are notoriously unreliable in their time of arrival, mothers-to-be are always advised to have their case packed for hospital well in advance of the Estimated Date of Delivery. It is better to err on the side of caution and have it ready too early than too late, because husbands are absolutely hopeless at finding all the right things after the event. However, those brides who take the hospital case on honeymoon are usually (though not always nowadays) being over-cautious.

Most hospitals issue a list of items that will be required. This is a typical example:

  2 cotton nightdresses   1 towel
  2 nursing brassieres   face cloth
  briefs (paper?)   soap
  dressing gown   tooth brush
  slippers   breast pads

To this list are frequently added:

  Money for telephone calls

Presents for elder siblings (if appropriate)
Salt (Well, it makes the food taste of *something*.)

Experienced campaigners will also include:

Ear plugs (All those babies)
Sleeping mask (All those nurses switching lights on at 6 a.m.)
Inflatable rubber ring (to sit on)
Radio (unless you can stand the intermittent reception of hospital earphones – and the fact that they're tuned to Radio Two all day)
Hay fever pills (All those flowers)
Bottle of Gin

There is one important and unalterable rule about the case for hospital:

EVEN THOUGH IT HAS BEEN TAKEN EVERYWHERE FOR AT LEAST TWO MONTHS, IT WILL ALWAYS BE SOMEWHERE ELSE WHEN THE LABOUR ACTUALLY STARTS.

(The only way for a mother-to-be to avoid this danger is for her to carry the case in her hand at all times. Not only will this ensure that she's ready when the labour starts, it will also quite possibly bring it on!)

CATARRH – According to most children, a musical instrument.

CATHETER – Name of a house owned by a rather twee couple called Peter and Catherine.

CATNET – a) With very small children, a device for keeping cats off the baby's pram (*See* Fig. 1).
b) With slightly larger children, essential equipment for a favourite game (*See* Fig. 2).

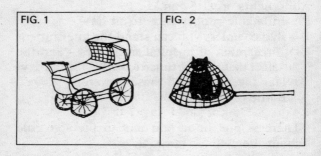

CAUTIONARY VERSES – These remain a popular method of entertaining children, while enforcing moral teachings. Unfortunately, many of the cautionary tales available concern such outdated hazards as Gas Balloons and Marble Busts of Abraham, which are not part of the day-to-day life of the modern child. To remedy this deficiency, here is a more up-to-date example of the genre:

IVOR BROWN

who placed too much Reliance on Mechanical Aids, and was put into an Institution.

IVOR BROWN, when a tiny Boy,
Was given an exciting Toy
By his oh! too indulgent Pater –
It was a Pocket Calculator.
The Lad took up the Gift with Glee,
And soon attained Proficiency
In working out what 87
Minus 3 and Plus 11,
Multiplied by .63,
Plus 12% of 8 would be
If it were divided by
Half of the Square Root of π
(And other Problems of that Kind,
Which so amuse the Infant Mind).
And, when he'd got the Answer, 'Crumbs!'
He'd cry. 'Oh, aren't I Good at Sums!'

He was – and yet it must be said –
He couldn't do them in his Head.
And when at School his Teachers tried
To show the Method, IVOR sighed
And sniffed and coughed and scratched his hair
And yawned and SIMPLY DIDN'T CARE!

It happened, though, a Ghastly Fate
Was stalking the Young Reprobate.
He went to spend his Christmas Loot
(A Five-Pound Note from Auntie Toot)
In a Large Department Store,
Picked up one Toy and wanted more,
So on his Calculator pored,
To see how much he could Afford.
He added up what he must Pay

And checked the Visual Display,
Which showed – to the Delight of IVOR –
That he'd spent Nowhere Near a Fiver!
He took more Toys and more and more,
As if he'd empty out the Store.
His Calculator favoured him; it
Showed him Nowhere Near his Limit!
So when he'd got all he could hold,
He went to the Check-Out and, as Bold
As Brass, he offered up his Fiver
To Pay for All – Oh! wretched IVOR!
He'd chosen to go into Town
The Day his Batteries ran down!

He might have Got Away With It,
If he had not been such a Nit.
The Check-Out Girl asked for more Money.
IVOR said, 'Now don't be funny.
Look – I've given you Five Nicker.
Give me my Change! Come on, Girl, quicker!'
The Girl refused, so IVOR swore,
Picked up his Toys, and left the Store.

The Magistrate, with Eye Severe,
Probationed him for Half a Year,
But IVOR went from Bad to Worse –
Stole his Probation Lady's Purse!
For which Society's Retribution
Put him in an Institution.
And there Poor IVOR, Sad to Say,
Remains until this very Day.

MORAL:
No Machine (of any Sort)
Will ever take the Place of Thought,
And Man – let it be widely known! –
Can't live by Microchip alone.

Cervix – The neck of the womb, which becomes distended during pregnancy and resumes its normal shape afterwards (*See Diagram*).

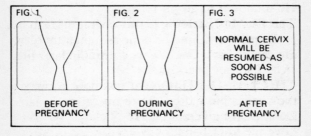

CHICKENPOX – A disease of promiscuous hens.

CHILDBIRTH – The most common form of birth in humans.

CHILD GUIDANCE – Usually a well-timed and well-placed slap.

CHILDHOOD – A garment to cover the head, decorated with bobbles and knitted by a spinster aunt, who hasn't seen a real child for years. (cf. MATINEE JACKET)

CHILDMINDERS - Most people mind children to a greater or lesser extent. Surveys have shown that the sections of the population who mind them most are fastidious bachelors with exquisitely furnished flats, and off-duty schoolteachers.

CHILD PSYCHOLOGIST - One who can tell you (frequently at considerable expense) why your child behaves appallingly, but not how to stop him.

CIRCUMCISION - If this operation is to be performed, it should be done as soon after birth as possible, as it can be very painful in later life.

CIRCUMSPECTION - Attitude with which the suggestion of the above operation in later life should be greeted.

COITUS INTERRUPTUS - The effect of children's Sunday morning television programmes finishing earlier than the parents had thought when they decided to have a lie-in.

COLIC - An Irish Christian name. (cf. THREE-MONTH COLIC – the son born to a trusting Irishman three months after he's finished a two-year jail sentence.)

COMFORTER - A dummy, soft toy, piece of material or bottle, from which an infant derives comfort by hugging or sucking. Often reliance on a comforter continues long beyond the infant stage (particularly when it's a bottle).

COMMON COLD – An infection caught by playing with children of inferior origins.

CONCEPTION – An idea. (Quite a good one, actually.)

CONSTIPATION – A no-go situation. (cf. DIARRHOEA – an ongoing situation.)

CONSULTANT – Someone capable of being more expensively ignorant of what's wrong with your child than your GP.

CONTRACTIONS – One of the first signs of a baby's arrival. The most notable are: contraction of space, contraction of social life, and contraction of the amount of spare cash around.

COUVADE – Sympathetic labour experienced by husband. In almost all cases stops short of actually having the baby.

CRACKERJACK SYNDROME – A disturbing condition which manifests itself in children who watch too much of a certain television programme. The first symptom is an awful banshee wail emitted at the mention of the word 'Crackerjack'. The second effect is even more disturbing; the child's sense of humour becomes crippled. It starts to believe that things which are totally unfunny deserve to be laughed at. Though some authorities maintain that this is a good training for viewing adult television comedy, it is still worrying. The only possible treatment is for the afflicted child to watch something that really is funny and hope thus to attain discrimination.

CRADLE CAP – Another of those inexplicable garments knitted by spinster aunts.

CRAVINGS – A very common female symptom. These are sudden desires for something totally irrational to be produced without delay. (Sometimes also evident during pregnancy.)

CRAVINGS–RECIPES – Pregnant women frequently find that they have overwhelming desires for unusual items of food, or conventional foodstuffs in unusual combinations (a phenomenon known as PICA).

Experienced mothers will be used to this, and stock their store-cupboards accordingly. But, for the less experienced, the following recipes will deal with most cravings:

1 DEEP-FROZEN FAGGOTS IN ICE CREAM
Take as many deep-frozen faggots as required, place them in a bowl of ice cream (ideally Raspberry Ripple), leave to soak for as short a time as possible, and then try to eat them.

2 CHERRY AND CHALK CRUMBLE

Take a pound of fresh, clean cherries. Stone them, and throw away the bits you don't want. Over the stones you have left, then crumble a lump of chalk. Serve at room temperature.

3 PILCHARDS CANADIAN-STYLE

Open a tin of pilchards (preferably in tomato sauce). Marinate overnight in Maple Syrup. In the morning go down to the kitchen and take a look at the result. (cf. MORNING SICKNESS)

4 CHARBON À L'EAU DE VAISSELLE PROVENÇAL

Select a sufficient number of bite-size lumps of coal. (If you live in a smokeless zone, Coalite or Homefire will do, though experts agree that the best flavour comes from real Nutty Slack.) Distribute the coal over the bottom of a circular cake dish, and brush lightly with washing-up liquid. For that authentic Provençal taste, add a clove of garlic, one well-crumbled Gauloise, and two teaspoonful of Ambre Solaire. Leave the dish in the middle of your dining-room table, and see how long it takes your craving to disappear.

CRAWLING – As soon as a child is seen to be crawling, the parent should ascertain what it's crawling with, and have it disinfected.

CREATIVE PLAY – See EGG-BOXES, TOILET-ROLL CYLINDERS.

CROSSWORD –
a) Expression of parental fury.
b) An ineffective device to keep the father-to-be's mind off things while his wife is in labour (*See Diagram*).

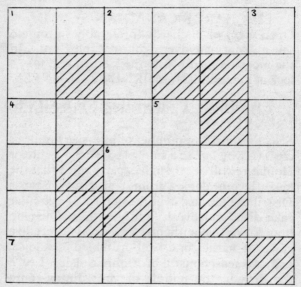

CLUES:

ACROSS
1 Sounds right in the best source of nourishment. (6)
4 Give birth to a cuddly toy? (4)
6 The seed was that started it all. (4)
7 Yah-boo! The baby does. (5)

DOWN
1 Labour's achievements. (6)
2 Estimated times of arrival in the East? (4)
3 Matching set of 1D. (5)
5 Music for the cradle. (4)

(For SOLUTION, see SOLUTION.)

CUDDLE – The most important single ingredient in a child's happiness (or an adult's).

DART METHOD OF FOLDING BABY'S NAPPY - *See Diagram.*

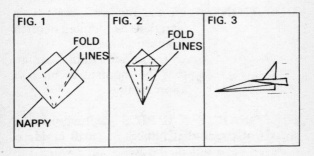

DELIVERY - This happens soon after the baby's birth (except during postal strikes); it is the arrival of the first batch of cards of congratulations.

   NORMAL DELIVERY: All the cards have got storks on them.

   ABNORMAL DELIVERY: Some of the cards haven't got storks on them.

FORCEPS DELIVERY: One of the cards has fallen into something unpleasant and has to be handled with care.

DEMAND FEEDING – When the mother wakes the baby up and demands that it be fed before she goes to bed.

DESTRUCTIVE CHILD – Any child.

DIAPER – An American nappy. No less dirty than an English nappy. (Even the Americans haven't found a way round that.)

DILATION – a) Of the mother's cervix – a sign that the moment of birth is approaching.
b) Of the father's pupils – a sign that the moment of birth is approaching.

DISPOSABLE NAPPIES – Unwholesome shreds of paper that fathers of small children have to poke out of the waste-pipe when the lavatory overflows.

DOT-TO-DOT PICTURES – These are a popular entertainment for young children, and also help the development of their co-ordination and numeracy. An outline of a picture is shown in numbered dots, and it becomes clear as the child joins up the dots in numerical order (*See Diagram*).

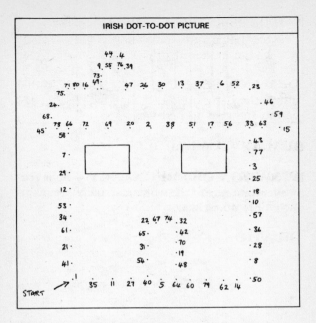

DRAW, LEARNING TO – A necessary part of the development of all children and cowboys. It tends to be a more destructive process with the former group. Cowboys learning to draw usually miss vital organs; no child armed with a sharp pencil ever does.

DRINKING – The instinct to swallow fluid is one of the earliest to develop and it continues strong throughout life (*See Diagram*).

DUMMY – A parent.

DURATION OF PREGNANCY – Believed by everyone except the woman actually pregnant to be only 40 weeks.

'EATING FOR TWO' – Sheer greed.

E.D.D. – Estimated Date of Delivery. (*See* LAST POSTING DATES FOR OVERSEAS SURFACE MAIL.)

EFFLEURAGE – A light, rhythmic massage, usually over the lower abdomen and back, with which husbands can successfully relax their wives before birth (and indeed before conception).

EGG-BOXES – *See* CREATIVE PLAY.

ELECTRIC BREAST PUMPS – There is a considerable variety of these on the market. Avoid those which are simply attachments to electric mixers, unless your baby shows an early predilection for milk shakes.

EMETIC – A stimulant to nausea (e.g. the news that it's going to be twins).

ENERGY – A phenomenon present in children, absent in adults.

ESTIMATING DELIVERY DATE – Human pregnancy is reckoned to last 280 days from the start of the last menstrual period, though the actual gap between conception and delivery is only 266 days.

From this it should be simple to work out the E.D.D. One method is expressed in this mnemonic verse:

FROM THE DATE OF THE START OF THE LAST PERIOD
   HAVING TAKEN THREE MONTHS,
SEVEN DAYS MUST THEN BE ADDED,
AND WHEN YOU'VE WORKED OUT THAT SUM,
   YOU'LL FIND YOU KNOW ALMOST AT ONTHS
JUST WHEN YOU'LL BE MUMMIED AND DADDED.

However, there are many factors confusing such calculations. These include:

A   Mothers reckoning they know best.
B   Mothers-in-law recognising 'a certain look in the eye'.
C   Husbands working it out with last year's diary.
D   Indigestion.
E   Sheer bad mathematics.

E.T.A. – Estimated Time of Arrival (Trains or Babies).

EVAPORATED MILK – Successful weaning.

EXERCISES, WHICH WILL PROVE USEFUL TO A NEW MOTHER.

(They may not do much for her figure, but the kids'll love watching her do them.)

FIG. 1 — THE HORSE (Useful for playing horses)

FIG. 2 — THE SIDE-BEND LIFT (Useful for opening cars' hatchback outside supermarket)

FIG. 3 — THE CROUCH (Useful for playing leapfrog)

FIG. 4 — THE WEIGHTS (Useful practice for carrying shopping)

FIG. 5 — THE SHOVE (Useful for pushing prams and negotiating supermarket queues)

FIG. 6 — THE MOVING CROUCH (Useful for entering Wendy houses)

FIG. 7 — THE CROSS (Useful for crossing the dining-room during children's parties)

FIG. 8 — THE FREE FALL (Useful practice for falling over unseen toys)

FIG. 9 — THE OSTRICH (Useful for pretending none of the whole ghastly business is happening)

EXPRESSING MILK – Feeding a baby in a hurry.

FACTS OF LIFE, EXPLAINING TO CHILDREN – It is never too early to start this process, though parents should be warned they are likely to encounter a certain amount of disbelief from younger children. It is probable that myths of storks and gooseberry bushes were created by parents as a defence against the hoots of derision with which the real facts were greeted.

FALLOPIAN TUBES – Tubes by which the ova are transported from the ovaries to the uterus (*See Diagram*).

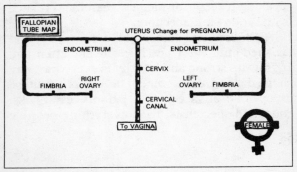

FALSE LABOUR – The main platform of every Tory election campaign.

FAMILY ALLOWANCE – Essential. Everyone should make allowances for people with families.

FAMILY PLANNING – Keeping rival grandmothers apart.

FEMALE – Peculiar to women.

FEMALE BEHAVIOUR – Peculiar to men (often *very* peculiar to men).

FINGER-SUCKING – An American expression.

FIRST AID – Mum.

FIRST WORD – The age at which a child speaks its first intelligible word varies enormously, and the definition of 'intelligible' depends on the indulgence of its parents.

One of the latest recorded instances of a child speaking (except for medical reasons) is related in the following anecdote.

'A mother and father had a baby boy, and lavished on it every possible care and attention. It grew up strong and healthy in every way, and showed good development in all its faculties, except that of speech. The parents read books, consulted specialists, tried everything possible to stimulate the child, but still it said nothing.

'This went on until the boy was five, when one day he sat down to lunch, watched by his adoring parents. He took a mouthful of his food, and then said, with perfect clarity, "There's too much salt in this."

'His parents were astounded. "Good heavens," cried his mother. "If you could talk like that all the time, why didn't you say anything before?"

'"Well, up until now," replied the child, "everything's been O.K."'

FISH FINGERS – What ever mother-to-be swears she will never give her children and what every mother very soon gives her children when faced with producing three meals a day for them (*See* BAKED BEANS).

FITS – What a child's hat rarely does.

FLAT FEET – A disorder of young mothers living in liftless apartment blocks.

FLUID INTAKE DURING PREGNANCY – Women should be persuaded to drink at least four pints a day during pregnancy. Their husbands are likely to do the same without persuasion.

FLYING DURING PREGNANCY – Very uncommon.

FLYING IN AEROPLANES DURING

PREGNANCY – More common, but to be undertaken with caution, particularly during the final months. Giving birth at 30,000 feet over the Galapagos Islands is never as glamorous as it looks in disaster movies. Besides, it gives the child a lifetime disadvantage when filling in 'Place of Birth' on forms.

FOETAL MONITOR – A senior embryo, who keeps the others in order.

FOETUS – Parents should be prepared for questions about the meaning of this word as soon as their children start school. It's only a matter of time before their puzzled infants will come home having sung in assembly:

> Leader, Seven Lee Father, leaders
> Or the worst impestuousy.
> Guarders, guiders, keepers, foetus,
> For we have no help but Thee.

FONTANELLE – The soft part in the middle of a baby's skull (known in adults as the BRAIN).

FOREIGN BODIES – Au pair girls (or boys).

FREE-WHEELING – According to a child, riding a tricycle.

FREQUENCY OF FEEDING BABY – This is something worked out between mother and child in the early months of their relationship. It takes a little while for the baby's demands and the mother's milk supply to adjust to each other, but it does happen eventually. The baby makes its demands known by crying and, once that starts, it's really a matter of how long the mother can hold out. There are variations between breast and bottle-fed babies, but the basic feeding and crying pattern of a 6-week-old baby is demonstrated in the following graph.

GRAPH OF EMERGENT MOTHER/BABY FEEDING RELATIONSHIP, AS AFFECTED BY INCIDENCE OF BABY'S CRYING AND FATHER'S BREAKING POINT, APPLIED TO BOTH BREAST-FED AND BOTTLE-FED BABIES.

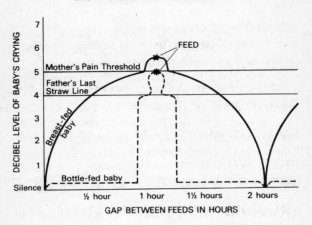

GAUZE – According to most children, a prickly bush.

GENES – These distinguish boys from girls (not to be confused with JEANS, which make boys and girls indistinguishable).

GENETICIST – One who can work out from a child's antecedents why he is as he is, but can't make him any different.

GENITALS, PLAYING WITH – This is a natural phase of development in all children (and adults) and should not be curbed. It is only when the children attempt to detach the genitals to play with them that parents should interfere.

GERMAN MEASLES – *See* RUBELLA.

GOOSEBERRY BUSH – To tell a child that babies are found under gooseberry bushes is a bad idea, because the child may subsequently appear from the garden carrying a worm and claiming it's its new brother.

GRIPE-WATER – A fluid whose purpose is to bring up the wind. Frequently used without success by Irish yachtsmen.

GUMS – Things that teeth are embedded into (available from all good confectioners).

GYNAECOLOGIST – A doctor to whom women can talk about ANYTHING (and EVERYTHING).

HAND-ME-DOWNS – Clothes passed down to a child from an elder sibling. This practice only causes problems when the children are of different sexes. Parents should be prepared for trouble from a little boy who doesn't like wearing his sister's dresses (or possibly more trouble, later on, from one who *does*).

HAT METHOD OF FOLDING BABY'S NAPPY*: *See Diagram.*

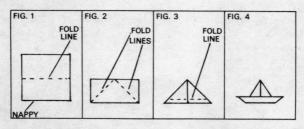

*(Also known as the BOAT METHOD. NB Boats made of nappies do not float very well. Nor, come to that, are hats made of nappies particularly comfortable.)

HEREDITY – The uncanny reappearance in children of all the good characteristics of one's own family and all the bad characteristics of one's in-laws.

HIGH CHAIR – A device to aid toddlers at meal times. The chair's elevation considerably increases the range over which they can throw food.

HOME CONFINEMENT – House arrest.

HOME PREGNANCY TESTING – There is a variety of methods available to the possibly expectant mother, some from chemists and some from folklore. As a general rule, it is prudent to avoid those which involve standing under Fairy Oaks at midnight or sacrificing frogs.

HUG – The most effective remedy for all childhood ailments.

IBEX – Word that occurs under 'I' in Children's Alphabets too sensitive to put 'Indian'.

INDEPENDENCE – A desirable quality which increases in children and diminishes in parents as they grow up.

INDUCTION OF LABOUR – A system whereby doctors and midwives get to see their favourite television programmes, have weekends and public holidays off. (A few years ago, had Jesus made a Second Coming, the practice would have ensured that he had to choose a different day from His first one.)

Induction has recently become less popular, because there are always risks attendant on interfering with the rules of nature.

Its main advantage is for parents who want to know exactly when their child is going to put in an appearance; induction gives them their first (and last) chance of such certainty.

INFANT HIVES – An experimental form of housing for small children, soon discontinued because the combs kept breaking and the honey got EVERYWHERE.

INSURANCE AGAINST TWINS – Precautionary policy taken out at huge expense by many expectant parents (except of course those who actually have twins).

INVERTED NIPPLES – Nipples that try to get milk out of the baby.

IPECACUANA – An emetic, not much used nowadays, because no one can pronounce it in the chemist.

IRON – A great help to the well-being of the pregnant and nursing mother.

IRONING – No help at all to the well-being of the pregnant and nursing mother. (*See* DRIP-DRY SHIRTS, YOU WON'T BE TAKING YOUR JACKET OFF ANYWAY, GRANNY'LL DO IT WHEN SHE COMES, etc.)

'IT'LL END IN TEARS' – The one invariably true axiom of childcare.

I.U.D. – Definitely NOT what Ian Smith once declared in Rhodesia.

JAUNDICE – Many babies become jaundiced soon after their birth, and this need not usually be any cause for anxiety, as it will soon pass. In the case of husbands who become jaundiced after the birth, the condition may last longer.

JELLY MOULDS – Jellies from ordinary moulds can be dull for children, because, when turned out onto plates, they are just shapeless blobs. To combat this dullness, manufacturers have produced jelly moulds in the shapes of rabbits, cars, trains, space-ships, etc. Their advantage is that jellies turned out onto plates from these moulds form different sorts of shapeless blobs.

JEWISH MOTHERS – Essential to the understanding of American television comedy shows.

JOINTS, MOVEMENT DURING PREGNANCY – Some movement of the joints is inevitable during pregnancy, but it should stop short of passing them round. (*See* SMOKING DURING PREGNANCY.)

JUMBLE SALE – Invaluable source of children's clothes, toys and germs.

'JUST LIKE' – One of the most common expressions in the upbringing of small babies. Usually occurring in sentences such as, 'Why, he's just like Uncle Reggie', it is a demonstration of a baby's remarkable ability to look exactly like half-remembered relatives on both sides of the family.

KICKING – A mother will be aware of her child kicking at various stages of its development, as follows:

1. KICKING AGAINST THE INSIDE OF THE WOMB – from the 18th week of pregnancy onwards till delivery.
2. KICKING AGAINST THE SHINS – from 2 years of age onwards.
3. KICKING OVER THE TRACES – from 2 years of age onwards ad infinitum.

KITE METHOD OF FOLDING BABY'S NAPPY: *See Diagram.*

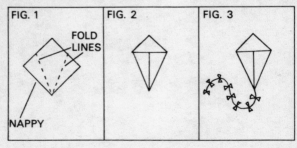

KISSING IT BETTER – A remedy for most children's injuries, whose undoubted efficacy is so far inexplicable to medical science (though recently a grant has been allotted for a Kissing Clinic at one of the major London teaching hospitals. As yet, no positive results have emerged from these researches, except for three marriages and seven engagements among the staff.)

KNEES – After the fifth month of pregnancy, women tend to lose sight of their knees. From then on, their husbands can help considerably by reassuring them that the knees are still there.

KNITTING – Knitting among potential grandparents is one of the first discernible symptoms of pregnancy. Any young wife who finds her mother or mother-in-law to be knitting should have a pregnancy test immediately.

LABOUR – The process of childbirth, so called because it's BLOODY HARD WORK.

LACTATION – The process of the manufacture of milk. (From the Latin *lac* – milk. Cf. GRAVITATION – the process of the manufacture of gravy.)

LAXATIVES – *See Diagram.*

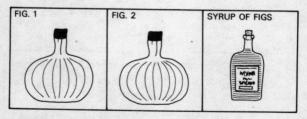

LAYETTE – A girl's Christian name, favoured by Country and Western singers.

LEBOYER METHOD – A method of childbirth, named after its French inventor, Charles Leboyer. Its approach is very gentle, relying heavily on building up a proper atmosphere, with soft lights and sweet music. Children born by this method tend to emerge from the womb smiling, dressed in white tie and tails and saying, 'Can I get you a drink, chérie?'

LEFT-HANDEDNESS – The tendency of a child to prefer to use its left hand at all times (except when being examined by a doctor for signs of left-handedness).

LIES – Parents get a lot of these once they have children.

LIE-INS – Parents don't get any of these once they have children.

LIMERICKS – There are surprisingly few limericks on the subject of childcare. This book, however, would be incomplete if it did not include a few examples of the genre.

A.

> A hand-grenade expert named Paul,
> Who knew nothing of babies at all,
>   Saw his son was unhappy,
>   Took the pin from his nappy,
> And threw the lad over a wall.

B.
> A breast-feeding mother who feels
> She must work to support her ideals,
>   Should get a job near at hand,
>   Buy some roller-skates, and
> Then can call herself 'Meals on Wheels'.

C.
> A Dad in the shower in the raw
> Saw his four-year-old come through the door.
>   When the youngster said, 'Cor!
>   Daddy, what are those for?'
> His father looked down and said, 'FOUR???'

LOCAL ANAESTHETICS – During LABOUR (q.v.), what many fathers resort to in the pub.

LULLABIES – Research has shown that the majority of parents are prepared to sing to their children to get them to sleep. (Mind you, research has shown that the majority of parents are prepared to do ANYTHING to their children to get them to sleep.) The majority of the parents who do sing tend to let out a meaningless drone ('Her-he-hum, her-he-hum der-de-dum, der-de-dum ...' ad infinitum or until the parent falls asleep), but some actually sing WORDS, and a few of these sing LULLABIES.

Since the stock of traditional lullabies is a bit meagre, here are some more modern examples of the genre:

TO BE SUNG BY FATHERS LEFT IN CHARGE OF BABIES OVERNIGHT:

Hush, little darling, don't wake up,
I've put some brandy in your cup,
And now I think I'll have some too,
So, if you should scream, I'll just
  sleep through!

TO BE SUNG BY MOTHERS IN HIGH-RISE FLATS:

Rock-a-bye baby
In the tower block.
When the wind blows,
The building will rock.
When the lift breaks
Is when Mummy swears,
Carrying baby
Up all those stairs!

TO BE SUNG BY THE TONE-DEAF:

Golden slumbers kiss your eyes,
Smiles await you when you rise.
Sleep, little darling, do not cry,
OR I WILL SING A LULLABY!!!

TO BE SUNG BY MOTHERS LEFT IN THE LURCH:

Bye Baby Bunting,
Daddy's gone a-hunting.
He's gone to buy a rabbit skin
To wrap his bloody mistress in!

MANUAL EXPRESSION OF MILK – *See Diagram.*

MASTURBATION – Hours of harmless fun.

MATERNITY CLOTHES – During pregnancy it is important for the mother-to-be to wear garments which are comfortable and do not restrict her movement. As the baby develops, so inevitably the mother's wardrobe must change (*See Diagram*).

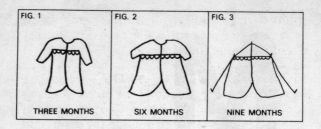

FIG. 1	FIG. 2	FIG. 3
THREE MONTHS	SIX MONTHS	NINE MONTHS

MATINEE JACKET – A garment of obscure function, knitted by a distant relative.

MBILICAL CORD – A misspelling of UMBILICAL CORD. (Also, incidentally, the name of a former Lord Chief Justice of Ghana.)

MEASURING JUGS – The best way of doing this is with a conventional ruler or tape-measure.

MEASURING SPOONS – Follow a similar procedure as in MEASURING JUGS.

MIXED FEEDING – To be encouraged. Segregating children of different sexes at meal times can lead to later abnormalities, like public school.

MIXED FEELING – Also to be encouraged. A perfectly normal (and continuing) stage of development in both sexes.

MOBILES – A young baby in a cot needs visual stimulation, and for this mobiles are ideal. They should flutter about in small circles over the cot, bobbing up and down with the wind. If you can't find a mobile, an unmarried aunt will often perform some, or in certain cases all, of the same functions.

MONTGOMERY'S GLANDS – These are situated on the areola round the nipple. During pregnancy, they become puffed up and, in extreme cases, want to go out into the desert and beat Rommel.

MORNING SICKNESS – A terrible sensation of nausea on waking up, an inability to cope with the day ahead and, commonly, actual vomiting at the thought of it. Frequently experienced by expectant fathers and, occasionally, expectant mothers.

MOTHERCRAFT – Mother supplied in kit form (liable to come unstuck).

MOTHER SUBSTITUTE – Scientists are still working on this, so far without success.

MOTOR ACTIVITIES IN YOUNG CHILDREN – Puking over car seats.

MUCUS – When a normal baby is born, there is mucus in its mouth, which the midwife will remove to facilitate breathing. When a very rich baby is born, she will have to do the same with the silver spoon.

MUMPS – A term of affection for a grandmother.

NAIL BITING – A symptom of nervousness manifested in children. It is bad for the teeth and doesn't do the nails much good either. *See also* FINGERNAIL BITING.

NAPPY PIN – A safety pin so designed that it never gets stuck into the baby, but almost invariably gets stuck into the thumb of the parent changing its nappy.

NATURAL CHILDBIRTH – A sequence of breathing exercises and little songs which give the mother-to-be something to do between the onset of labour and surrender to the epidural.

NIPPLE SHIELDS – Plastic contraptions worn by pregnant women, which get them funny looks from people they accidentally brush against in crowds. (NOTE TO HUSBANDS SENT OUT TO BUY NIPPLE SHIELDS:

Be prepared for the question, How many do you want? The answer is not always as obvious as it might seem.)

NITS – a) Small lice which infest children's hair.
b) Parents who believe they only occur among the lower classes.

NUDITY – There is nothing shocking about nudity. Mind you, it can be quite funny.

NURSERY RHYMES – Nursery Rhymes have traditionally been used extensively for the education and amusement of children, and it is only in recent years that they have come under fire for being out of touch with modern life and, in particular, for perpetuating outdated sexual role stereotypes. To avoid such dangers, many traditional rhymes have been amended to conform with modern thinking.

In some cases, the minimum of change is required to avoid sexism, as in this example:

> Personbird, personbird, fly away home:
> Your house is on fire, your children are gone.

Other rhymes need a more basic alteration to remove unwelcome overtones, as in:

> What are little boys made of?
> What are little boys made of?
> Just the same as little girls.

But in most, the spirit of the original can be maintained and simply modernised to fit in better with current thinking. For example:

> Curly locks, curly locks, wilt thou be mine?
> Thou shalt not wash dishes alone, nor feed swine.
> I'll help thee clean and wind thy wool;
> Our relationship will be meaningful.

Or again:

> Georgie Porgie, pudding and pie,
> Kissed the girls and made them cry.
> Just self-gratifying he,
> Georgie Porgie's an M.C.P.

This modernising process is very important for the children who are going to be brought up on nursery rhymes and will prevent them from thinking that their parents and teachers have lost touch with modern life. Here are two more, more general examples:

> There was an old woman who lived in a shoe;
> She had so many children she didn't know
>   what to do
> She went to the council, destitute,
> And they rehoused her in a boot.

And finally:

> One misty, moisty morning,
> When cloudy was the weather,
> There I met an old man
> Clothed all in leather.
> Clothed all in leather,
> With cap under his chin –
> I remembered mother's warning
> And took no sweets from him.

NURSING BRA – A contraption of hooks and laces, not dissimilar to a cricket pad.

OBSTETRICIAN – A doctor who has the same skills and four times the salary of a midwife.

OLD WIVES' TALES – Anecdotes regularly produced in any discussion of children's illness or behaviour, all beginning with the words, 'We had just the same trouble with ours ...'

ONE-WAY NAPPY LINERS – No nappy liners work more than one way. That way is by slipping round so that the really noxious bits of mess end up on the nappy itself. (*See* FALLING BETWEEN TWO STOOLS.)

ORAL CONTRACEPTIVE – A 99 per cent infallible method. If the woman talks *enough*, the man will eventually go to sleep.

PAEDIATRICIAN – One who specialises in disorders of children. (cf. COMPREHENSIVE SCHOOL TEACHER, RIOT CONTROL POLICE, etc.)

PAIN IN THE BACK – A common symptom of pregnancy.

PAIN IN THE NECK – Someone who keeps complaining of the above.

PELICAN BIBS – Plastic bibs with a curled-up tray at the bottom to catch food. These represent a challenge to the creative child, who will go to considerable lengths to ensure that most of his or her food misses the tray.

PERSONALITY CHANGES DURING PREGNANCY – It certainly does.

PERT – An expression used by parents to

describe the behaviour of a child beginning to develop its own identity.

PETHIDINE – A pain-killer much used during labour. Though sometimes useful, it has the disadvantage of making the mother so drowsy that she may not notice she's had the baby (or care much, come to that).

PFANNENSTEIL INCISION – Also known as BIKINI CUT. A form of Caesarian operation, whereby a horizontal rather than a vertical cut enables the mother to wear a bikini afterwards (if she isn't too embarrassed about her size and stretch-marks to wear one anyway).

PHANTOM PREGNANCY – Imaginary pregnancy. It rarely goes the full nine months, but, if it does, is less likely to produce a boy than a ghoul.

PHENERGAN– A drug used by parents to sedate overactive children, to counter the syndrome known as PHENERGAN'S WAKE.

PHOTOGRAPHS OF CHILDREN – All parents want to make a record of the development of their offspring, and, since children make very good subjects for the camera, photographs of them proliferate in most households. However, there is a marked change in the volume of photographic records taken of the first, and of subsequent children (*See Diagram.*)

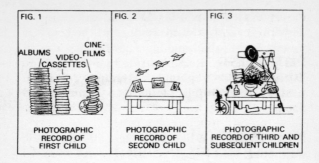

FIG. 1	FIG. 2	FIG. 3
PHOTOGRAPHIC RECORD OF FIRST CHILD	PHOTOGRAPHIC RECORD OF SECOND CHILD	PHOTOGRAPHIC RECORD OF THIRD AND SUBSEQUENT CHILDREN

PIGEON TOES – What will the children's food manufacturers think of next? *See* FISH FINGERS.

PILL – a) Contraceptive.
b) Travel sickness.
(Heed the example of the woman who got the two sorts mixed up – she had fourteen children and her husband could never get the car started.)

PLACENTA – A Play Centre run by trendy Hampstead feminists.

PLASTICINE – A multi-coloured, pliable modelling medium, which one day's handling by a child reduces to hard brown lumps.

PLASTIC PANTS – But only after very heavy exercise (cf. METAL FATIGUE).

PLAYING WITH FOOD – All children play with their food at some stage, and the sensible parent, rather than making a conflict issue of it, will play along. Recommended games include Diced Mixed Vegetable Monopoly, Ravioli Ludo, Game Chip Roulette, Backgammon, and Sardines.

PLAYPEN – What scribbles all over new wallpaper.

PLAYTHING – The diversion of a few minutes for a child, soon to be rejected as too boring (e.g. a parent).

POSSET – A small amount of vomit from a baby, not sufficient to upset the child, but sufficient to make the parent change the garment on which it landed.

POSTNATAL EXERCISES – *See Diagram.*

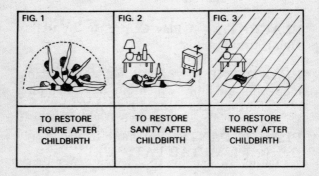

FIG. 1	FIG. 2	FIG. 3
TO RESTORE FIGURE AFTER CHILDBIRTH	TO RESTORE SANITY AFTER CHILDBIRTH	TO RESTORE ENERGY AFTER CHILDBIRTH

POWDER, MILK – Just add water to make milk.

POWDER, WATER – Just add milk to make milk.

POWDER, BABY – Just add water to make a baby. (This version of the Facts of Life is not recommended to any parent, however embarrassed about the subject.)

PREFERENCE FOR ONE BREAST OVER THE OTHER – Unusual. Most babies (and men) prefer them side by side.

PREGNANCY TESTING – Yes, it is, very.

PRESENCE, MOTHER'S AT BIRTH – Recommended by all authorities.

PRESENCE, MOTHER'S AT CONCEPTION – Again strongly recommended.

PRESENCE, FATHER'S AT CONCEPTION – Assumed in all the best circles.

PRESENCE, FATHER'S AT BIRTH – Increasingly fathers-to-be are encouraged to be present at the moment when they cease to be 'to be' and become the real thing. Many fathers-to-be appreciate this, on the principle that they like to see through anything they've started.

Fathers-to-be in the Labour Ward can

perform a variety of more or less useless functions. Of these, probably the most useless is mopping their wives' brows with cologne-soaked handkerchiefs. Sometimes their presence is valuable to the wives because they can be given shopping lists, instructions as to how the washing machine works and advice on how to make a workable truce with the wife's mother who is arriving shortly to look after the house.

But the greatest value of a husband in the Labour Ward is that his rolling eyes, greenish tinge and trembling hands tend to make the wife feel better. Under the circumstances, it's obviously not the comfort of knowing there's someone worse off than she is, just the satisfaction that at least the bastard's suffering a bit.

(Another very important recommendation to doctors and midwives for the husband's presence is that it gives the wife someone else to swear at during the transitional stage of labour.)

Where the husband stands during labour is important. Obviously, as a totally useless object, he must not get in the way of any of the medical staff. The diagram below offers some suggestions.

PRIMIGRAVIDA – Woman expecting first child.
ELDERLY PRIMIGRAVIDA – Woman over 35 expecting first child.
UNLIKELY PRIMIGRAVIDA – Woman over 55 expecting first child.

PROJECTILE VOMITING – One of the earliest games for babies. They score 1 point for hitting their bib, 2 for their own clothes, 5 for their parents' clothes, 7 for the carpet, and 10 for a direct hit on the new three-piece suite.

PUERPERAL –
a) Relating to childbirth.
b) A child's spelling of the colour it gets by mixing red and blue.

PUSH – An unanswerable exhortation vehemently repeated to mothers at the climax of labour and fathers at the swings.

PUSHER – An implement with which a child can push food onto its spoon (i.e. a Finger).

PUTTING THINGS AWAY – Extensive tests have revealed this to be the one activity of which no child is capable.

QUARANTINE – The period during which a disease is infectious. It varies between one day and six months, according to which other mother the mother of the sick child last spoke to on the phone.

QUESTIONS – One of the most virulent of childhood diseases. Tends to become chronic if treated with ANSWERS.

QUICKENING OF FOETUS – In a normal pregnancy the foetus quickens at about eighteen weeks. But it doesn't quicken that much; there's more than as long again before it deigns to emerge.

QUIET – Essential for the pregnant or nursing mother. Usually obtained by repeated loud shouts of 'QUIET!!!'

RASH – Having another baby.

RATTLES – As children soon find out, anything does if you bang it on the table long enough.

REGISTERING A BIRTH – There is never any problem about this. Unless unconscious, the mother usually registers a birth as soon as it happens.

REGURGITATION – A long word for something everyone knows by a much shorter word.

RELIEF BOTTLE – A bottle to be used for comfort if the baby's mother is unavoidably absent. If the father's left in charge, it usually contains whisky.

REST – Recommended for expectant mothers

and frequently obtained during first pregnancy, when husband is touchingly solicitous and there are no other children in the house. In subsequent pregnancies, FORGET IT.

ROMPERS – A trendy Mayfair discotheque.

ROUND-SHOULDERED – Many children are round-shouldered. This is quite normal and you should not worry about it. Only if your child is oblong or triangular-shouldered should you start to worry.

ROUND SHOULDERS – A malformation which manifests itself soon after a baby's birth – in the child's father. Some fathers develop it even earlier, in fact as soon as they get married.

RUBBER SHEETS – Protective coverings that invariably wrinkle up down the middle of the bed, enabling the child to pee either side of them.

RUBELLA – *See* GERMAN MEASLES.

RUNNY NOSE – The inevitable attribute of any child who wants to give you a big kiss.

RUSKS –
a) Hard biscuits to help a child who is teething.
b) Soft biscuits left in the oven by a mother who has had to go and help a child who is teething.

SECOND BABY – What arrives just when you think you've finally got the smell of nappies out of the house, and brings it straight back again.

SEX BEFORE PREGNANCY – Essential.

SEX DURING PREGNANCY – Ask your doctor. If he's not interested, ask your husband.

SEX AFTER PREGNANCY – Essential.

SEX DETERMINATION – What the father always feels when the mother is most tired.

SEX PLAY – 'O Calcutta!'

SINGING TO SLEEP – Rendering insensible by musical means. (*See also* MAX BYGRAVES, DES O'CONNOR, BARRY MANILOW, etc.)

SITTING UP – There are considerable variations in the times at which individual children will sit up. The only generalisation one can make is that they never do it when you're trying to get a T-shirt over their heads.

SLEEP – For parents, a childhood memory. For children, an unwelcome interruption to everything else.

'SLEEPING LIKE A BABY' – Snorting, snuffling, grunting, farting, and waking every two minutes to scream.

SMARTIES – The ultimate weapon in all negotiations with children.

SMILING – After about six weeks babies will often smile at their parents. Thereafter they become more discriminating.

SMOKING DURING PREGNANCY – Extremely unlikely. It is not a symptom that has ever been observed in pregnant women.

SNIFF – What a child does when a handkerchief is put to its nose and it is told to BLOW.

SNOT – Childish expression of disagreement.

SOCIAL ATTITUDES TO CHILDREN – Britain is still a very class-ridden society, and attitudes to various aspects of childcare vary from class to class. Even individual words and sounds take on different meanings according to who's using them – as can be demonstrated by the following glossary:

SOUND	LOWER CLASS MEANING	MIDDLE CLASS MEANING	UPPER CLASS MEANING
AUNTIE	Any female adult whom the child meets regularly.	Sister or sister-in-law of parent.	Sister or sister-in law of parent, invariably titled, whose name the child has been given, in hopes that it will clean up from the aunt's will.
BET	A daily flutter on the horses.	A modest investment on the Grand National and Derby.	What the son of the house will learn to play cricket with.
CHIPS	Staple food for children.	French fried potatoes.	Gaming counters.
CLIMATE	What you do with your Family Allowance.	What may affect your child's health when on holiday.	What one does to a mountain (because it's there).
CRECHE	Never heard of it – our Nan looks after the baby.	Communal baby-care facility.	A car accident.

SOUND	LOWER CLASS MEANING	MIDDLE CLASS MEANING	UPPER CLASS MEANING
NANNY	Grandmother.	a) Girl who helps with child while mother is out working, has best room in the house, colour TV, boyfriends who drink husband's Scotch, and is paid more than mother earns. b) Female goat for those with dreams of self-sufficiency.	Norland-trained girl who ensures that mother need not be aware that she has a baby.
ORAL STIMULATION FOR BABY	Dummy in mouth.	Nipple in mouth.	Silver spoon in mouth.
PEER GROUP	Members of coach-trip to Southend.	Children of the same age.	The House of Lords.
PREM	Never heard of it.	Born before term.	A perambulator.
ROLLS	Bread-cakes, filled with ham, cheese, etc., for children's tea.	Parts played by participants in parent/child relationships.	Family runabout.
UNCLE	Any male adult whom the child meets regularly.	Unfamiliar man found by child in mother's bed	Brother or brother-in-law of parent, etc. (See AUNTIE.)
WAIF	Homeless child.	Homeless child.	Lady to whom gentleman is married.

SOUND	LOWER CLASS MEANING	MIDDLE CLASS MEANING	UPPER CLASS MEANING
WAYNE	Commonly, a child's first name.	Commonly, a surname.	Commonly, a present laid down for a new baby boy by an indulgent godfather.
WINDSOR	Enquiry (usually in compound – 'Windsor bloody kid gonna stop crying?')	Site of a safari park, popular with children.	Surname of distant relatives.

SOCIAL WORKER – Someone who knows better than Mum. (cf. ANTISOCIAL WORKER: Someone who tells Mum she knows better than Mum.)

SOLIDS, INTRODUCTION INTO BABY'S DIET – It should never be forgotten that the introduction of solids into a baby's diet also means the introduction of solids into a baby's nappy.

SOLUTION –
a)   Sodium hypochlorite and water, used cold as a sterilising medium.
b)   To crossword (*See Diagram*).

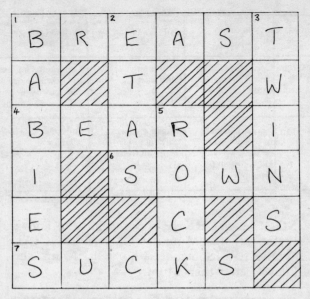

SPOCK, DR – Guru of childcare specialists. On the whole, very sound, though some of his ideas are a bit weird (possibly due to Venusian ancestry and funny ears).

SQUINTS – Almost all squints in children can now be corrected by therapy or surgery. The only kind that cannot is shown in Fig. 3 of the diagram below.

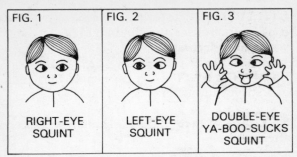

FIG. 1	FIG. 2	FIG. 3
RIGHT-EYE SQUINT	LEFT-EYE SQUINT	DOUBLE-EYE YA-BOO-SUCKS SQUINT

STANDING, DEVELOPMENT OF – The emergence of a child's ability to hold itself upright exactly between its father's favourite armchair and the television screen.

STERILISATION – Recommended for bottles after heavy use and parents after even heavier use.

STOOLS – Things that babies sit on.

STORK – The theory that storks deliver babies has been disproved by practical experiment (*See Diagram*).

FIG. 1	FIG. 2	FIG. 3	FIG. 4
STORK BEFORE EXPERIMENT (Very cheerful, because of lucrative margarine advertising deal)	BABY BEFORE EXPERIMENT	BABY AFTER EXPERIMENT	STORK AFTER EXPERIMENT (Now reduced to doing Concorde impressions)

STRAWBERRY MARK – The inevitable consequence of serving children's tea in a room you've just decorated.

STRETCH SUIT – Any garment in the hands of a strong and determined child.

STYES – Where children should be placed after meals.

SUPPLEMENTARY FEEDING – The habit among small children of coming into their parents' beds on Sunday mornings and eating the newspapers.

SURGICAL SPIRIT – Medical enthusiasm for Caesarian delivery.

SUTURE – From the Latin word meaning 'to sew'. Chiefly used by mothers in the expression 'Suture self, you little sew-and-sew!'

SWADDLING – It is important for children to know the meaning of this word; otherwise they will never understand Christmas carols.

SWALLOWING PATTERNS – Only to be expected if you leave them lying around where the baby can get at them.

TAKING A CHILD'S TEMPERATURE – This has traditionally always been done with a glass thermometer, either in the mouth or rectum. Recently, however, a simpler device has appeared on the market, in the form of a plastic strip to be placed on the forehead. Skin temperature will cause a letter to be clearly readable on the strip, to show whether or not there is any danger (*See Diagram*).

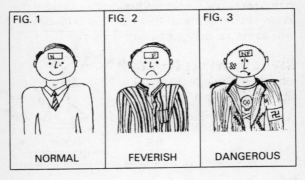

TALKING – Parents spend the first two years of their child's life desperately teaching it to talk, and the rest regretting it ever learned.

TASTE, CHANGES IN, DURING PREGNANCY – Many women find that pregnancy affects their tastes. They feel an unexpected, but total, revulsion for things which previously gave them pleasure (e.g. coffee, oranges, rare beef, husbands).

TEATS, ARTIFICIAL – These come in a variety of styles and it is important that every mother should choose the one that suits her child. The following illustrations may make that choice easier.

FIG. 1	FIG. 2	FIG. 3
THE COMMON TEAT	THE TEATIME SPECIAL	THE TEATOTAL
FIG. 4	FIG. 5	FIG 6
THE TEAT-A-TEAT	THE PETEAT	THE NEFERTEATI

TEETH – A child develops a variety of teeth as it grows up, and it is important that its parents should recognise the different sorts (*See Diagram*).

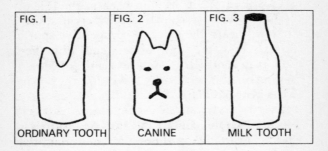

FIG. 1	FIG. 2	FIG. 3
ORDINARY TOOTH	CANINE	MILK TOOTH

TEETHING – *See* WIND.

TELEVISION, INFLUENCE OF – Television is a fact of life for modern children, and parents who try to stop their children from seeing it might as well be trying to stop them from growing up. No parent need ever worry about his or her child watching too much television. It is ultimately a very boring medium and, since children are very intelligent, they will ultimately realise this (though it may take them a lifetime to do so).

However, until that time comes, it is important that they should have television available. This will help them to cope with many problems at school. They will realise that other children who walk around saying 'Crackerjack' or 'Hong Kong Phooey' are neither foreign nor mentally defective. They will realise, if hit by another child, that he did it because he was Batman saving civilisation as we know it, and not because he was a vicious little sod (and so feel justified in hitting him back in the rôle of the Joker, out once again to destroy civilisation). They will learn the value of competitive sports (though they may not understand why they can't play football dressed as giant policemen floating on huge water-lily leaves like they do in 'It's a Knockout').

TELEVISION, EDUCATIONAL INFLUENCE OF – Television has an undoubted educational influence. Many children's programmes teach small children how to use their hands and make useless artefacts out of cotton reels, egg boxes, washing-up liquid bottles and toilet roll cylinders. This means that every household under the influence of such programmes is littered with loose cotton, eggs, washing-up liquid and toilet paper, which have all been removed to provide the raw materials of creativity. (If the programmes viewed are on the B.B.C., parents will also find that their offspring have gone around putting masking tape over the trade names on all the bottles, boxes, etc. that they use.)

Though it is hard sometimes to see the practical value of these creative activities, it is important to remember that we are approaching a time of dwindling natural resources. The ability to recycle cotton reels, egg boxes, washing-up liquid bottles and toilet roll cylinders may prove to be exactly the sort of skill the next generation will require.

TELEVISION, INFLUENCE ON LANGUAGE – *See* BLUE PETER SYNDROME.

'THANK YOU FOR HAVING ME' – A polite child's response to:
a) A host or hostess.
b) Its mother.
c) A boy or girl friend. (This applies only to *older* children.)

'THREE-MONTH COLIC' – An attack of colic which keeps a baby awake for one night, but which seems to its parents to go on for three months. (*See* COLIC.)

TINNED BABY FOODS – There are many of these on the market, exotic combinations of such delights as Liver and Carrot, Beef and Spinach, Ham and Prune, etc. The only thing they have in common is that they all taste like soggy cardboard.

TOILET ROLL CYLINDERS – *See* CREATIVE PLAY.

TOILET TRAINING – An impossible feat. Toilets cannot be trained to do anything.

TOOTH FAIRY – Woe betide the father and mother who do not make contact with this sprite when their children lose teeth. Since the first tooth usually comes out after the child has started school, there is no escape from paying the going rate, as the child will be well briefed on the subject by its contemporaries.

(FORMULA FOR WORKING OUT THE GOING RATE FOR THE TOOTH FAIRY'S SERVICES, PER UNIT TOOTH:

Let 'a' be the amount the parent feels inclined to pay. ('Pity they don't make threepenny bits any more.') Let 'b' be the highest amount the child asserts any of his or her contemporaries have attained. ('When Emma lost her first tooth, the Tooth Fairy put a pound under her pillow.')

$$\text{THE GOING RATE} = \frac{b - a}{9}$$

NB Under all circumstances, ensure that the Tooth Fairy TAKES AWAY the tooth from under the pillow when substituting the money. There is no child so virtuous as to be above trying the trick two nights running.

TOURNIQUET – Something which stops one's circulation – like, for example, having a baby.

TRAINING PANTS – Sounds emitted by children after vigorous sporting activity.

TRANSITION – That part of labour (q.v.) between the First (q.v.) and Second (q.v.) Stage (d.v.), when the woman may lose control and start swearing at anyone present, particularly her husband. (A phenomenon also observed in women who aren't even pregnant.)

TRAVEL TO HOSPITAL – The onset of labour gives every father-to-be the opportunity to drive like something out of a car chase from an American movie. If stopped by the Law, he has the unanswerable excuse, 'My wife's in labour', and usually gets a police escort rather than a summons.

Unfortunately, many fathers-to-be find that when their moment comes, they have no chance to show off their dare-devil skills, because there is no traffic on the roads and all the lights are in their favour. But, for dreamers, the map below shows what can be done. (The course of the father-to-be's car is shown by the line of arrows.)

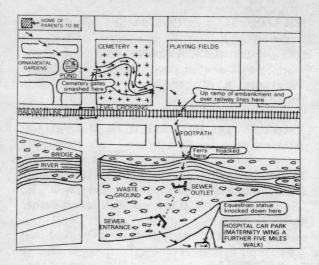

TRIMESTER – One of the three three-month phases of pregnancy, and not, as it sounds, a new aid to slimming.

TRIMNASTICS – A course of exercises to keep women in leotards and in shape – ideal for restoring the figure after childbirth.
(Not to be confused with:

SLIMNASTICS: A course of exercises to help women fit into their leotards.
VIMNASTICS: A course of exercises to help women in leotards enjoy cleaning the bath.
GRIMNASTICS: A totally exhausting course of exercises for women in leotards.
HYMNASTICS: A course of exercises to keep

women in leotards on the straight and narrow.

PRIMNASTICS: A course of exercises for women who don't think it's nice to wear just leotards.

OR,

WHIMNASTICS: A course of exercises which women in leotards stop doing when they think of something else.)

TRIPLETS – Three children at one birth. Likely to cause problems, particularly in Ireland, where the father may well set off with a shotgun, looking for the other two men responsible.

ULTRASOUND – Really wild in-womb entertainment for the switched-on foetus.

UNDERWEAR, SUITABLE FOR MOTHERS-TO-BE – The various stages of pregnancy require different sorts of underwear (*See Diagram*).

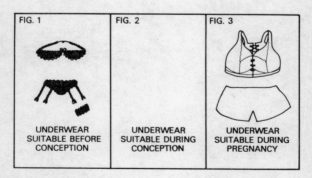

FIG. 1	FIG. 2	FIG. 3
UNDERWEAR SUITABLE BEFORE CONCEPTION	UNDERWEAR SUITABLE DURING CONCEPTION	UNDERWEAR SUITABLE DURING PREGNANCY

UNIOVULAR TWINS – Identical twins, born from the separation of a single egg. (For advice on how to separate an egg, consult MRS BEETON'S BOOK OF HOUSEHOLD MANAGEMENT.)

URINE TEST – This is the most common way of diagnosing early pregnancy. If positive, the result will reveal in the specimen the presence of chorionic gonadotrophin. If negative, the result will be much easier to pronounce.

VARICOSE VEINS – Unsightly blue bumps seen on other people's legs.

VIRUS – Any illness for which there is no entry in this book.

VITAL STATISTICS – A woman's vital statistics are markedly changed by pregnancy (*See Diagram*).

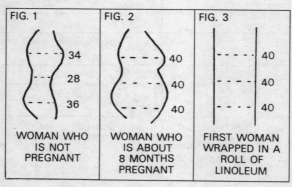

VITAMIN TABLETS – These are manufactured to make people cheerful and full of well-being. Tests have proved beyond doubt that the purchase of such tablets does make their manufacturers cheerful and full of well-being.

VOCABULARY, DEVELOPMENT OF – A recent study by a group of academics who had nothing better to do with their grants came up with the following results, demonstrating the vocabulary used by male of the species to get what it wants:

AGE	NOTES	VOCAL EXPRESSION
1 month	Very small	Waaaaaaa!
6 months	Still pretty small	Waa-waa-waa!
1 year	A bit bigger	Ug...?
1½ years	,,	Gug-gug...?
2 years	,,	Want!
2½ years	,,	Me want!
4 years	,,	I want!
5 years	A very brief period.	Please may I have...?
5¼ years	At school.	Gimme!
18 years	Dating	Go on. It'll be all right. Honestly.
23 years	Newly married	Come on, darling... Ooh... aah...
30 years	After some years of marriage and children.	Ug...?

VOICE, BREAKING – A condition occurring in adolescent boys and overwrought mothers.

'WANDERING EYE' – A phenomenon observed in many newborn babies (and their fathers).

WARBLE – Something a child asks for to keep it warm in bed. (Sometimes HOT WARBLE.)

WARTS – Very common in children from the age of two onwards. Particularly in the sentence, 'Warts that?'

WATERS BREAKING –
a) A sign of the onset of labour.
b) A sign that Moses has been at the Red Sea again.

'WHAT DO YOU SAY?' – A risky way of eliciting the words 'Thank you' from a child who has been given something. It all too often prompts the answer, 'Can I have another one?'

WHERE TO HAVE YOUR BABY – There is a lot of nonsense talked about this. When it comes down to it, except in the case of Caesarian delivery, all women have their babies from the same place.

WIND – *See* TEETHING.

WORKING MOTHER – Any mother.

XYLOPHONE – Word that always occurs in Children's Alphabets under 'X'.

YIPPEE!! – Sound emitted by husband on hearing that all is O.K. at wife's six-week post-natal check-up.

ZEBRA – Word that always occurs in Children's Alphabets under 'Z'.

APPENDIX I – NAMING YOUR CHILD

The choice of a child's name is of paramount importance (or at least plaza importance), because it is something that will stay with the child all through life. And discussing names for their potential offspring is a harmless way in which parents can while away the weary months of pregnancy.

Many factors influence the choice of names: considerations of class (e.g. Gervase, Humphrey, Devereux, Runtinghorn), considerations of another class (e.g. Tracey, Joylene, Rayette, Duane, Wayne, Daryl, Clint), ethnic origins (e.g. Hamish, Cadwallader, Oonagh, Chlodowig, Onuphrious, Fagin), the cycle of fashionable preoccupations (e.g. Zak, Sunflower, Zowie, Ecology, Cannabis) and, most important, what's on television (e.g. Ena, Fleur, Mork, Esther, Reginald, Meg, Paddington, Roobarb).

Other important considerations are: not offending either side of the family and therefore including unlikely names of grandparents, etc. (*See* FAMILY PLANNING q.v.), and using names of extremely rich and distant relatives, who might possibly be sentimental (or senile) when making their wills.

The basic test for any name is to bawl it at the top of your voice. Imagine its owner has just poured boiling hot custard over the cat in the middle of the new dining-room carpet (as, in time, it will), and really let rip. It is amazing how quickly this method reduces the number of names on your shortlist.

Other important considerations are, of course, sex (make sure you have a supply of names ready for both eventualities) and the possibility of multiple births (a *big* supply of names).

But there are still many pitfalls for the unwary parent. Remember, your child will not just be known by its Christian name, but by its Christian name *in conjunction* with its surname. The following list can aid your selection. If your surname appears in the left-hand column, avoid the Christian name in the right-hand column.

SURNAME	CHRISTIAN NAME TO BE AVOIDED
Balls	Ophelia
Bedd	Aneurin
Beeker	Philippa
Boots	Sonia, Ulick
Brick	Eva
Buckett	Kika
Cake	Henrietta
Cart	Orson
Case	Justin
Down	Enoch
Dresden-Spatz	Natalie
Gonne	Chastity, Honour, Modesty
Hopeandglory	Orlando
Hyde	Tanya
Inch	Colum

SURNAME	CHRISTIAN NAME TO BE AVOIDED
Kettle	Lydia
Lamb	Sean
Minor	Maurice
Mower	Lorna
Over	Saul
Quirke	Ivor
Ranger	Ilona
Rolls	Ham
Rolls-Royce	Iona
Round	Wanda
Sandwich	Lettice, Salome
Seville	Barbara
Shutt	Isadore
Tickett	Raphael
Wetherall-Followe	Clement
Widdle	Mustapha
Work	Rudyard

Though much of this might appear to be common sense, it is surprising how often unfortunate accidents of nomenclature still arise. Even parents who take great care over the juxtaposition of their child's Christian name and surname, can come unstuck *when the Christian name is shortened*. The ensuing list will assist parents in avoiding that particular pitfall:

SURNAME	CHRISTIAN NAME THAT SEEMS O.K.	ABBREVIATION THAT ISN'T O.K.
Banks	Robert	Rob
Behan	Lesley	Les
Bird	Dorothea	Dolly
Brush	Lewis	Lew
Coe	Bronwen	Bron
	Henry	Harry
Furse	Constance	Connie
Gonne	Pauline	Polly
Hart	Richard	Dickie
Ibbett	Henry	Hal
Legge	Margaret	Peg
Mander	Sarah	Sally
Minor	Miriam	Minnie
Pickles	Dilys	Dil
Sandwich	Janet	Jan
Scarfe	Edward	Ed
Side	Reginald	Reggie
Sleigh	Robert	Bob
Slipp	James	Jim
Spitz	Nathan	Nat
Taylor	Jennifer	Jenny
Tickell	Theresa	Tess

But, even after taking all the above precautions, parents can still condemn their children to a lifetime of being sniggered at by injudicious choice of middle names. Some initials can ruin otherwise perfectly acceptable combinations, as:

SURNAME	CHRISTIAN NAME	OFFENDING MIDDLE INITIAL
Bottoms	Nicole	S.
Bough (pron. Boff)	Evan	C.
Clare	Wally	D.
Cross	Sheila	B.
Dunn	Esther	B.
Fore	Seamus	B.
Gee	Rhoda	G.
Gee-String	Aaron	A.
Going	Vera	V.
Goodness	Shirley	T.
Knott	May	B.
Lord	Titus	A.
Melody	Dick	C.
Poe	Sybil	I.
Saltz	Barbie	Q.
Side	Hugo	N.
Twomey	Wallis	N.
Williams	Denis	E.
Zoff	Nick	R.

Considering the many pitfalls possible, it is not surprising that many parents fall back on names which show no originality at all. (And, if your name's Bates and you're expecting a child, pray it's a girl, so that it doesn't have to suffer the stage of being called Master.)

APPENDIX II

AT-A-GLANCE FAULT DIAGNOSIS CHART
(Applicable to all cases of child malfunction, except for genuine illness)

FAULT IN CHILD	CAUSE	PARENT'S REMEDY
Total Deafness	Child has just been asked to tidy up.	a) Loom over child until it does tidy up. b) Give up the unequal struggle and do it yourself.
Total Blindness	Child has been asked to go upstairs and fetch something from bedroom.	No point in persevering. Go up and get it yourself.
Total Dumbness	Child has been asked to say, 'Thank you for having me.'	Wait. It may take some time, but wait.
Child is covered in red spots.	Child has been playing with mother's lipstick.	Remove spots with a tissue (or don't bother – they'll wear off eventually).
Child is covered in multi-coloured spots.	Either, as above (depends on mother's taste in lipstick), or child has been eating Neapolitan ice-cream.	Soap and water.

FAULT IN CHILD	CAUSE	PARENT'S REMEDY
Child has gone white around the mouth.	Child has been licking out the last bit of a sherbet dab.	Soap and water.
Child's teeth have turned black.	Child has been eating liquorice.	Toothpaste, soap and water.
Child clutches bottom and looks anguished.	Child has torn brand new trousers.	Admonition, serious talk about cost of children's clothes, needle and thread.
Child has dramatically high temperature.	Child has been secretly putting thermometer on hot water bottle or central heating radiator.	Send child back to school, even though it's rice pudding day.
In the middle of a game, child suddenly falls down, clutching shin and screaming.	Child has been watching too much football on television.	Ignore.
Child takes on ferocious expression and tries to tear clothes.	Child is playing the Incredible Hulk.	Discourage from tearing clothes, otherwise ignore.

Also in Unwin Paperbacks

FAVOURITE NAMES FOR BOYS AND GIRLS
Patrick Cook

Did you know that **Susan** has its origins in ancient Persian drinking songs, that **David** means 'no sheep is safe', that **Felicity** comes from a Latin term meaning 'very rich parents', and that all **Dawns** go into dry cleaning?

Favourite Names for Boys and Girls is an invaluable guide to all new parents, interfering relatives and everyone else faced with the important question 'What shall we call Baby?' or 'What do I really mean?' In this book are hundreds of answers, including a comprehensive list of historical origins, nicknames, key physical characteristics and likely occupations.

MORE FAVOURITE NAMES FOR BOYS AND GIRLS
Patrick Cook

Did you know that **Graham** is a geological term? That **Glenn** means 'hole in the ground'? That **Bronwen** means 'rich in fibre'?

More Favourite Names for Boys and Girls is a companion volume to the internationally well-received *Favourite Names for Boys and Girls*. It is an indispensable guide for newly blessed parents, their relatives, popular novelists and others in search of just the right name; or those who are concerned about their own identities. Hundreds of choices are offered, vigorously researched and historically sound, with particular attention to likely physical peculiarities and areas of employment.

QUOTE ... UNQUOTE
Nigel Rees

Aphorisms and apothegms, bons mots and bromides, epigrams and epitaphs, repartees and rejoinders, squibs and squelches, wise saws and wisecracks – that is the stuff Nigel Rees' radio series 'Quote ... Unquote' is made of. Part quiz, part anthology, the 'Quote ... Unquote' book deliciously captures its flavour. There are catchphrases and spoonerisms, famous first and last words, Sam Goldwynisms, Dorothy Parkerisms, Margot Asquith's brilliant 'margots' and the gaffes, goofs, immortal and mortal remarks of Prime Ministers, Presidents, film, radio and TV stars, and all sorts of other people.

'a great hit ... packed with entertaining quotes and quizzes' *Daily Mirror*
'Hilarious' *Evening News*

QUOTE ... UNQUOTE 2
Nigel Rees

This new compendium contains the immortal musings of kings, presidents and menu-writers, legendary crossword clues, hilarious newspaper headlines and rare jokes from the Bible. A host of steamy sayings proves there's more to sex than just doing it. Stolen titles and scrambled sayings test your knowledge of quotations and throughout the book there is a generous sprinkling of 'unquotes' – quotes that have been tampered with, stood on their heads and put to other uses their makers never dreamed of.

'That great rarity, a witty quiz book' *Now*
'A magical formula ... sheer entertainment'
Yorkshire Post

Also in Unwin Paperbacks

Babes and Sucklings *Nigel Rees*	£1.50 ☐
Graffiti 1 *Nigel Rees*	£1.50 ☐
Graffiti 2 *Nigel Rees*	£1.50 ☐
Graffiti 3 *Nigel Rees*	£1.50 ☐
Graffiti 4 *Nigel Rees*	£1.50 ☐
Favourite Names for Boys and Girls *Patrick Cook*	£2.50 ☐
More Favourite Names for Boys and Girls *Patrick Cook*	£2.50 ☐
The Jaws of Sex *Tony Pinchuck*	£1.95 ☐
Last Laughs *Russell Ash*	£1.50 ☐
Last Will and Testament *Richard De'ath*	£1.50 ☐
Nigel Rees Book of Slogans and Catchphrases	£2.95 ☐
Odd Idioms *Erica Bendix*	£1.95 ☐
Quote … Unquote *Nigel Rees*	£1.50 ☐
Quote … Unquote 2 *Nigel Rees*	£1.50 ☐
Tombstone Humour *Richard De'ath*	£1.50 ☐

All these books are available at your local bookshop or newsagent, or can be ordered direct by post. Just tick the titles you want and fill in the form below.

Name ....
Address ....
....
....

Write to Unwin Cash Sales, PO Box 11, Falmouth, Cornwall TR10 9EN.
Please enclose remittance to the value of the cover price plus:
UK: 55p for the first book plus 22p for the second book, thereafter 14p for each additional book ordered to a maximum charge of £1.75.
BFPO and EIRE: 55p for the first book plus 22p for the second book and 14p for the next 7 books and thereafter 8p per book.
OVERSEAS: £1.00 for the first book plus 25p per copy for each additional book.

Unwin Paperbacks reserve the right to show new retail prices on covers, which may differ from those previously advertised in the text or elsewhere. Postage rates are also subject to revision.